Go for Liftoff!

How to Train Like an Astronaut

Dave Williams, MD, and Loredana Cunti
art by Theo Krynauw

 annick press
toronto + berkeley + vancouver

Contents

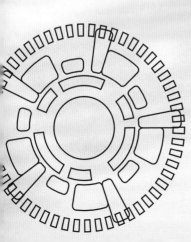

Step 4: Basic Training

Step 5: Your Mission Is Go!

Welcome from Dr. Dave

Passion, commitment, persistence, and optimism are all part of the astronaut attitude. It's about learning to be your best and enjoying the journey of pursuing your dreams.

Dr. Dave Williams

Exploring scuba diving

Astronaut survival training

Skydiving

Exploration has always been my passion. When I was seven years old, I watched the first NASA astronauts fly in space and I knew I wanted to be an astronaut. My journey began at age twelve when I learned to scuba dive, which showed me how the body works in unique environments. That led me to a career in science and medicine, and eventually to becoming an astronaut. It is never too early to believe in yourself, push your limits, and reach for your dreams.

So You Want to Be an Astronaut

Do you wish you had a space suit in your closet? Do you dream of traveling in a rocket ship? Can you picture yourself floating high above Earth? News flash: YOU WANT TO BE AN ASTRONAUT.

And really, who wouldn't? Exploring space is one of the coolest jobs on—or off—the planet. If you like science, taking on challenges, and learning new and amazing things, keep reading!

Being an astronaut is awesome, but it doesn't come easy. You've got to work to make your dream a reality—and that's exactly where things get interesting. In this book, you'll learn just what it takes to have a truly out-of-this-world job. So, are you ready to train like an astronaut?

Hi Mom, gonna be late for supper tonight!

Dr. Dave goes through wilderness-survival training.

It's Not All Rocket Science

Learning to be an astronaut isn't just about science and space travel. Before they are sent to space, astronauts have to go through spacecraft systems training, wilderness training, underwater training, roller-coaster-like flight training, teamwork training, and, of course, science, technology, medical, engineering, and math training. That's a lot of training (and a lot of tests!). But as any astronaut will tell you, the gain is totally worth the pain!

Astronaut Samantha Cristoforetti learns how to operate an IMAX camera.

Rocks, Docs, and Space

So, what if you dream of snorkeling instead of space? Rocks instead of rockets? Never fear: not all astronauts start out with an interest in space. A passion for something totally different can still lead up, up, and away!

Taking Stock of Rock

Geologists are scientists who study the materials that make up Earth, like rocks and minerals. This is especially important for answering questions about the origins of our solar system. Does a rock or soil sample from Mars show any signs of having supported life?

NASA's Curiosity Mars rover

Scoop marks in the sand on Mars

Swimmers for Space

What does scuba diving have to do with space? Because floating under-water is a lot like floating in space, astronauts do a lot of training in pools and the ocean. So, if you want to be an astronaut, scuba skills are required.

Call the Doctor!

Doctors know how the human body works when it's healthy, when it's sick or hurt, and when it's under "extreme" conditions. Whether high in the mountains, deep in the ocean, or way out in space, an expert in the medicine of extreme environments is always good to have around.

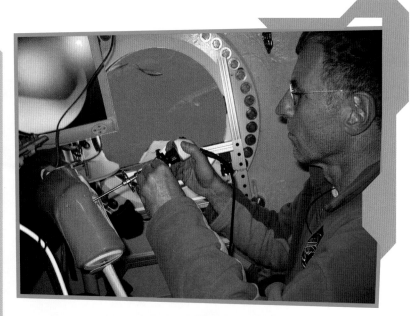

Dr. Dave performs a surgical simulation in the Aquarius underwater laboratory.

Planetary Pilots

Test pilots fly new aircraft (and spacecraft, too) to make sure the vehicles perform well and are safe. If things go wrong, be prepared to eject!

Captain Brad Matherne does a preflight check before a training mission.

Develop Your
Astronaut Attitude

Going Up?

Whatever gets you dreaming about space, the first step in your astronaut training is an attitude check.

Astronaut Wannabe Checklist

At space camp, kids get to feel what gravity is like on the moon.

✔ Curiosity

It turns out curiosity is more important than rocket fuel. What's really out there? Does space go on forever? Astronauts want to know! Without curiosity, humans would never have walked on the moon. Will Mars be our next stop?

✔ Confidence and Physical Fitness

Confidence means believing in your own abilities—even when you're doing things that are tough.

8

Passion

Passion is that feeling you get when you love something *so much* that you want to do it all the time. Your passion might be soccer or reading or video games. An astronaut's passion is exploring space.

Resilience

Resilience is dusting yourself off and getting back on when you fall off your bike. Trying new things is hard! Remember that you won't succeed at everything you try, and certainly not right away (and if you do, it probably means you're ready for the next step). You can learn a lot from failure.

Commitment means hard work and practice.

Commitment

Saying you love baseball and then skipping practices is the opposite of commitment. But scheduling enough rehearsal time to make sure you ace your piano exam? That's true commitment. Astronauts show commitment by constantly challenging themselves to be the best they can be.

It's what we do when we don't succeed that determines whether or not we do succeed.

No "I" in Team

Astronauts work and live together for months at a time. On the International Space Station (ISS), there could be five crewmates—from at least two different countries—sharing a mission with you. Do you have what it takes to get along?

Expeditionary Behavior Basics

Your classroom probably has a "code of conduct"—something you reviewed on your first day of school to make sure everyone is on their best behavior. Astronauts have a code, too—it's called "expeditionary behavior." A mission to Mars might last three years. Who wants to spend that much time with a person who complains all day or eats the last snack without sharing? You can get a head start on your expeditionary behavior training by

* putting mission goals and others first (maybe your "mission" is a class project)
* treating everyone the way you'd like to be treated
* helping others to succeed
* being humble

Steady!

Working as a team

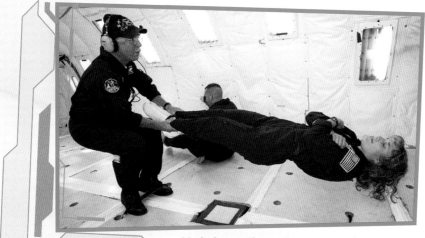

Helping others to succeed

* being kind and openhearted
* sharing and taking care of your stuff
* being honest, responsible, and accountable
* admitting to mistakes and apologizing
* welcoming differences
* being positive

Debrief on Differences

Are all of your classmates from the same place? No way! Some were born in other countries, some are part of a different culture, and some speak another language. But you all have to communicate and get along. That's good practice for astronaut training!

Put the Cool in School

Whys and Hows

Science, math, technology, health, language, geography—pretty much every school subject can lead to a future in space travel. The key is to never stop exploring new areas of interest. Luckily, school is the perfect place to ask questions and find answers!

Kindergarten (ages 4 and 5):

Time to learn your ABCs and 123s.

Elementary School (ages 6–13):

Time to ask "Why?" Why is the sky blue? Why can't we breathe underwater? Why do I have to eat broccoli?

High School (ages 14–17):

Time to ask "How?" How does gravity work? How did we discover the planets? How soon will I be able to drive?

A love of science can lead to a future in space exploration.

College/University (ages 18–21):

Time for bigger questions: How does the human body repair itself? How do we build strong and stable bridges to drive on? What do I want to be?

I loved science throughout school–especially doing experiments–but I knew I wasn't the smartest kid in the class.
In university, I wanted to be a doctor but I still wasn't the smartest kid. With a lot of hard work, I won a gold medal in medical school that I later flew in space!

Dr. Dave began doing experiments at a young age.

What's Next?

So you've graduated from college or university. Excellent! But if you want to be an astronaut, you're not done with school yet. Good thing you're curious, because there's still so much to learn!

More University (ages 21–25):

Let the fun begin! Whether you want to spend your time experimenting in a laboratory, exploring the underwater world, or learning how planes are built and how they fly, "graduate school" (where learning takes place after you already have a college or university degree) is where you get to really focus on what interests you.

Teams compete at NASA's Sample Return Robot Challenge.

Becoming a field scientist is good training.

Do What You Love (age 25 plus):

Once you are *finally* done with school, it's time to get a job, probably in science, medicine, technology, engineering, arts, or math. And if you're still dreaming astronaut dreams, it's time to start doing what you love to do—in space. Get ready for your astronaut application!

Astronaut candidates are usually between 26 and 46. The average age is 34. I was 38 and working as an emergency doctor when I filled out my application.

Terrestrial Tryouts

Space Agencies Want You!

There are tryouts for all kinds of clubs and teams: the baseball team, the gymnastics team, the chess club, and the lead in the school play. Space agencies hold tryouts too—for astronauts! If you've completed your schooling and have been doing your job successfully for a few years, *or* if you have been flying a high-performance airplane for the right number of hours, you can apply to be an astronaut.

In 1992, when I applied to the Canadian Space Agency, there were over 5,000 applicants. Around 600 were from kids under 10 years of age. Maybe there should be a space program for kids!

APPLICATION FOR THE ANTI-GRAVITY ADVENTURER

My name is

I am   years old

I am good at

I want to be an astro

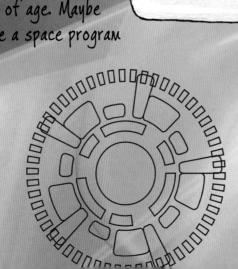

THE SPACE PROGRAM

APPLICATION FORM   1A

NAME : .....Moon Rover.....
AGE : 5 dog years (35 human)
HEIGHT : 3½ feet
WEIGHT : 42 pounds

EXPERIENCE :
Obedience school, 4 years paper delivery.
Ate Meg's science homework.

SKILLS :
Retrieving, digging, advanced physics.

INTERESTS : Nature, space, ball.

Astronauts Are Everywhere!

The United States has NASA (the National Aeronautics and Space Administration); Canada has the Canadian Space Agency; and a bunch of countries work together in the European Space Agency. But they aren't alone. Here are just a few of the many other countries with astronaut training programs:

* Russia
* China
* Japan
* India

In space, we don't see country borders. We're exploring on behalf of the whole planet.

The international crew on Dr. Dave's NASA space mission

Intergalactic Interview

You aced your written application—whew! Next up is a face-to-face meeting. Because so many people want to become astronauts, space agencies are *really* picky. They separate the all-star candidates from the just-okays with interviews and background checks. Time to make a good first impression!

Being a good team member

Attitude for High Altitude

Want to plan ahead for your astronaut interview? Think about these questions:

* Why do you think you would make a good astronaut?
* Can you give an example of when you were a good teammate?
* Can you keep working while you're throwing up? (Warning! Astronauts often get sick during microgravity training.)
* What do you do when things don't work out the way you planned?

Checking You Out

Space agencies also run background checks on astronaut candidates. They might call your friends and family, your teachers, or your boss. Why? They need to be sure that

* you are who you say you are
* you do not have a damaging history (such as a criminal record or a really bad social media site)
* the information you included on your application is true (like where you went to school and what jobs you've had)

Barbara Morgan, former teacher

Dr. Chiaki Mukai, former surgeon

Dr. Rick Linnehan, former veterinarian

Free-Float Fitness

Interview: check! Background check: check! But you're not done yet. Prepare for the Astronaut Physical and Swim Test. You can't get to outer space if you're not fit for a spaceflight, and you can't perform underwater zero-gravity training if you can't swim!

Weightless Well-Being

Have you ever noticed that your first sports practice of the season is the hardest? That's because you're probably a little out of shape after some time off. Astronauts don't let themselves get out of shape. For them, being fit is a way of life. It can be for you, too. Be active every day, eat healthy, and get the right amount of sleep. You'll fly through your physical if you start now!

Astronaut Terry Virts trains in the Partial Gravity Simulator.

Astronaut Eileen Collins lowers herself from a simulated shuttle.

Exercising for endurance

Cardiovascular exercise

3, 2, 1 . . . Go!

An astronaut needs three types of exercise:

* **Cardiovascular:** Keeps heart and lungs ready for peak performance. Who knows when you'll have to get back to the air lock—fast.
* **Endurance:** When the going gets tough, the tough keep going. If you're 10 kilometers (6 miles) away from your planetary habitat and your rover breaks, you're walking back!
* **Strength training:** Resistance training with weights helps build muscles and strength. In space, objects (even weights!) don't have weight, so astronauts use bungee cords for resistance instead.

NASA's John Glenn flew his second spaceflight at 77. He couldn't have done that if he hadn't stayed in tip-top shape.

Basic Training

You Can ASCAN

"Congratulations! You've been accepted to the space program." Time to celebrate—and get busy! You'll be moving to the town where the space agency is located so you can officially start the Astronaut Candidate training program.

Welcome to Class

At NASA, Astronaut Candidates—ASCANs, in space speak—get selected into a "class." Each class is given a number based on the year they begin training, but that's boring, right? Astronauts want cool names for their class, so they come up with nicknames. Check out these: 8 Balls, Chumps, Peacocks, Bugs, Penguins, Sardines, Flying Escargot, Hogs, and Hairballs. Not exactly scientific!

Astronauts Michael Fincke and Drew Feustel get ready to train underwater.

If at First You Don't Succeed ...

With only a few spots available and thousands of people applying, you might not get chosen on your first space agency application. That's okay. If you keep trying—and challenging yourself—you will have a better chance of getting there. The astronaut's approach is simple: practice until you get it right and then push onward!

After countless hours of practice, astronaut Joan Higginbotham prepares for a flight.

APPLICATIONS

NASA's 2011 call for new astronauts received 6,100 applications for only 8 spots! A request for applications in December 2015 resulted in over 18,000 responses.

Astro-Class

Wondering how you can possibly learn all the stuff you need to know to go to space? You go to school! The ASCAN training program helps you develop the knowledge and skills you'll need to succeed.

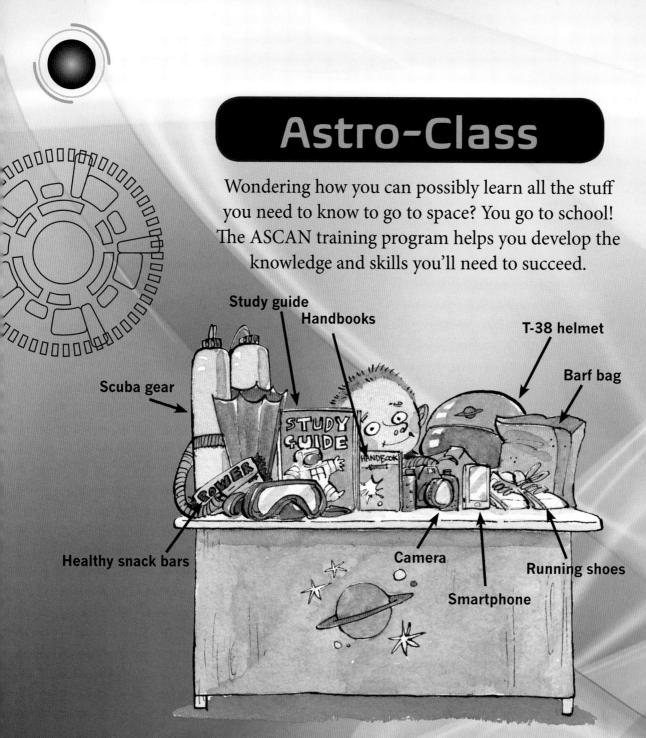

Study guide

Handbooks

T-38 helmet

Barf bag

Scuba gear

Healthy snack bars

Camera

Smartphone

Running shoes

The official languages of the ISS are English and Russian. These days, astronauts launch into outer space from Russia's Baikonur Cosmodrome. If you want to say "Hello, cosmonauts!" get out your dictionary!

Learning for Liftoff

ASCANs spend about two years discovering what it's like to live and work in space. Training covers everything from expeditionary behavior and teamwork to spacecraft systems and flying high-performance jets. Other subjects include

* space walking
* robotics
* space science
* life science
* first aid and CPR
* engineering
* astronomy
* scuba diving
* Russian

Underwater training for
planetary space walks

Dr. Dave flying a
high-performance jet

T-38 jet used in
flight training

Putting the STEM in SySTEM

Have you ever heard your teacher talk about STEM (short for science, technology, engineering, and math)? Astronauts know all about STEM. A lot of it went into creating the systems that make life in space possible. ASCANs spend hundreds of hours learning how these systems work.

What Makes a Rocket Move?

Spacecraft use propulsion systems—a series of powerful rocket engines—to make it to the Moon and back (or anywhere else in space). Propulsion systems use a force called *thrust* to move the rocket through space. If a thruster is fired in one direction (down), the spacecraft will move in the opposite direction (up)! Propulsion systems also power the special backpacks sometimes used during space walks.

The Soyuz rocket is propelled up into space.

Hot and Cold

Space suits are high-tech heating and cooling systems, designed to keep astronauts comfortable. Each one comes with multiple layers, including long underwear. Add a bit of body heat and it gets toasty in there. Thankfully, the suit's liquid cooling garment helps sweat evaporate, lowering the temperature inside and preventing the visor from fogging up.

No Plugs?

How do you get power when there are no plugs in space? The ISS's electrical power system converts energy from the sun (solar energy) into power for lights, equipment, and onboard computers. "Power connectors" do the same job in space as plugs do on Earth.

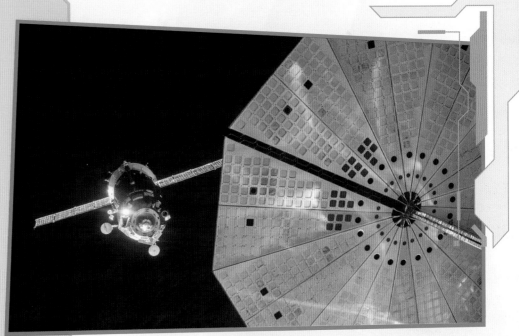

Solar energy powers the ISS.

A Need for Speed

Speaking of systems, rockets wouldn't be able to get to or stay in outer space without some serious systems in place. While the propulsion system keeps the spacecraft moving forward, the guidance and navigation systems tell it where to go. (If you can't work the GPS in the family car, you'll want to pay extra attention in that class!) Astronauts need to understand all of that, and, of course, they need to be comfortable with speed …

Mach Masters

Astronauts travel at 25 times the speed of sound—or Mach 25. Spaceflight readiness training—a big part of basic training—takes place in supersonic jets. To join the Mach masters club, you need

* outstanding eye-hand coordination
* the ability to handle many tasks at once
* knowledge of onboard computers and flight systems
* the ability to communicate with air traffic control
* the ability to work effectively with your teammates
* practice time on a supersonic jet

DC-9 diving
toward the Earth

Roller-Coaster in the Sky

ASCANs use a DC-9 airplane to learn about free-floating in microgravity. After climbing super high, the pilot pushes the plane into a dive. Then the astronauts are in free fall—and they float around, just like in space. After 20 seconds, the plane pulls out of the dive, climbs back up, and starts again. No wonder it's called the "vomit comet"!

Astronaut candidates in free fall

Fly higher than 80 kilometers (50 miles) above Earth and you can officially call yourself an astronaut!

Get Your Hands on This!

You might have guessed by now that astronaut candidates have *a lot* of hands-on training. On top of hundreds of hours of classroom training, you'll practice for hundreds of hours on simulators—machines designed to let you experience what it's like to live and work in space.

Practice Makes Perfect

In space, astronauts have what's known as "zero error tolerance." That means no mistakes! But we all make mistakes, right? That's why astronauts train as though they're *in space*. They practice basic skills (like going to the bathroom in the space toilet simulator) and very complex skills (like docking their spacecraft to the ISS). Simulators provide a safe place where ASCANs can make mistakes and learn from them until they get it right.

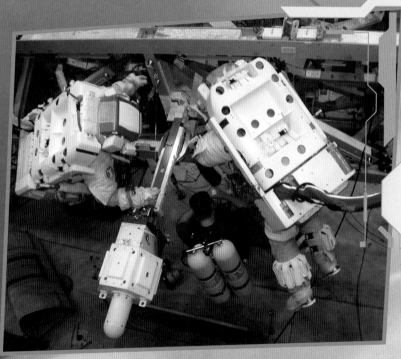

Dr. Dave and Clay Anderson practice space-walking skills underwater.

Off Nominal? Uh-Oh!

All space missions have at least two highly skilled pilots on board, but sometimes things still don't go according to plan. "Off nominal" is astronaut code for "something's not right." Technology helps out in these situations, but you still need to know what to do. Good thing you didn't snooze through training!

Astronauts Mark Kelly and Gregory Johnson in the motion-based shuttle mission simulator

Astronaut Chris Ferguson takes part in a de-orbit training session.

Super-Cool Simulators

Check out just a few of the simulators ASCANs get to practice on during basic training.

Down to Docking

A fixed-base simulator helps ASCANs learning how to dock. Docking your spacecraft is kind of like parking your bike in the garage—if your garage was moving away from you at the same time! You don't want to hit the side of Mom's car or smash into the tool shed. Now imagine parking your bike while traveling at 25 times the speed of sound!

Space crew practice docking with the ISS in the Systems Engineering Simulator.

Rocky Rocket Ride

A motion-based trainer simulates the noise, vibrations, and views that astronauts experience during shuttle launch and landing.

The motion-based trainer is my favorite simulator, especially when we're wearing our orange launch and entry suits. It's a great reminder of what it's really like in space.

Home Sweet Hatch

Spacecraft don't have doors between compartments; they have hatches. If something goes wrong with the air pressure in one module—making it unsafe for astronauts—the hatch creates a seal. Hatches are important during space walks, too, when the inside of the spacecraft needs to be safely sealed before the outside doors are opened. Knowing how to open and close a hatch can be the difference between life and death. No wonder there's a simulator for that!

Very funny, let me in guys! ... Guys?

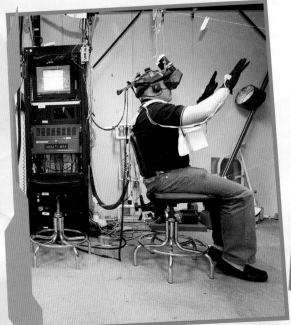

Astronaut Greg Chamitoff goes through virtual reality training.

The Altitude Chamber Complex simulates a space environment.

Astronauts participate in an emergency training session on a full-scale simulator.

The Pool Rules

Imagine a backyard pool more than half the size of a football field! That's the Neutral Buoyancy Laboratory (NBL)—the world's largest indoor pool. But this pool's not for swimming. It's where astronauts train underwater for space walks.

Gravity Game

During underwater training, ASCANs wear full space suits—and weights. Too few weights and you float to the surface; too many and you sink. When the weights are just right, the feeling of floating deep in the pool is as close to a space walk as you can get on Earth. In training for a mission to the Moon or Mars, where the gravity is different, the weights are adjusted so it feels just like being there.

Astronaut Tracy Caldwell Dyson takes part in an underwater space-walk training session.

Difference with the Dive

There's one big difference between underwater training and an actual space walk. In the NBL, the water all around you makes it hard to start moving but easy to stop. In space, it's easy to start but really hard to stop. Move too quickly "up there" and you might just smash into the space station. Ouch!

Astronauts Terry Virts (left) and Samantha Cristoforetti train underwater to prepare for work on the outside of the ISS.

Coastal Choreography

Astronauts spend about 10 hours walking underwater for every hour they spend walking in space. They also develop "choreography" (just like in dance class) for every space duty. It's not easy to pick up a tool when you're wearing a space glove!

Swimming with the Fish

When it comes to preparing for long missions on the ISS, ASCANs move from the pool to the ocean, where they can live for up to three weeks. The Aquarius Reef Base—the world's only undersea research laboratory—is located on a reef, off the coast of Florida, 18 meters (60 feet) under the surface of the ocean.

Astronauts in training arrive at the Aquarius underwater laboratory.

Pressure at Your Porch

After diving down to the habitat, ASCANs enter through an open "wet porch"—no hatch required. That's because the air pressure inside Aquarius is kept equal to the pressure supplied by the ocean. Not only does that make it safe to breathe, it also prevents seawater from getting in.

It's easy to get lost when living or working underwater (especially in the dark!). Ropes suspended about 3 meters (10 feet) off the reef have arrows pointing to the habitat. And at night, the lights inside guide aquanauts home.

Underwater Work

Aquarius can be an ASCAN's home for up to three weeks. You'll wake up, eat meals, exercise, and do experiments in the habitat—just like on the ISS. By adding weights as you walk on the sandy reef outside of the habitat, it is possible to recreate the gravitational environment of the Moon or Mars. And when it's time to do research or practice mission training, you'll swim out to the nearby reef. Wave to the fish on your way to work!

Aquanaut Josef Schmid watches a grouper swim by a window of his undersea home.

Astronauts practice simulated space moves on the ocean floor.

Orbiting the Great Outdoors

Do you like camping, foraging for food, and building fires? Good! In addition to their training in and around the water, today's astronauts also learn how to survive in the great outdoors, in every season.

Why Wilderness?

If wilderness training seems odd for astronauts, just think about what could happen in an "off nominal" situation. What if you touch down in the wilderness, far away from where you were supposed to land? Wilderness training lets astronauts learn and practice survival skills, on their own and with their crewmates.

Astronaut candidates Tyler Hague (left), Andrew Morgan (center), and Nicole Mann (right) take part in wilderness training.

It Could Happen to You!

In 1965, the crew of the Russian Voskhod 2 mission learned exactly why wilderness training is a good idea. Their spacecraft guidance system broke and they landed in the snowy forests of Siberia, about 2,000 kilometers (almost 1,250 miles) from the targeted landing site. They spent a cold night huddled in the capsule with bears and wolves right outside.

Wilderness-Survival Training Checklist

Learn how to
* catch and eat bugs
* build a snow cave
* fend off wolves
* start a fire in the rain
* get safe drinking water (even from a muddy puddle!)

Astronaut Joseph Acaba collects water during ASCAN land-survival training.

Calling All Astronauts

How did you do? Did you pass your basic training with flying colors? Congratulations, grad! You are an official astronaut! Now it's time to get assigned to a mission.

Missions Accomplished!

There have been some amazing space missions over the past 50 years. Here are just a few:

* Neurolab: helped scientists understand how the brain and body adapt to space.
* Spacelab and SPACEHAB: created a research laboratory in space. (Dr. Dave flew on both of these missions!)
* Space Shuttle/Space Station: used the Space Shuttle to bring new modules to the space station.
* Soyuz/Space Station: brought humans to and from the ISS.
* Hubble: replaced parts of the Hubble telescope with newer ones to fix the focus and keep the images of deep space sharp.

What amazing things will tomorrow's astronauts accomplish?

Soyuz TMA-7 on its way to the ISS

Astronaut Story Musgrave (top) prepares to place new parts on the Hubble telescope.

Silver Solar Surfer

At your basic training graduation ceremony, you're presented with a silver astronaut pin. This pin was designed by some of the first humans whose mission was to travel to outer space. They were called the NASA Mercury astronauts. The Mercury missions were named after a Roman god known for his incredible speed.

Silver astronaut pin presented at graduation

Astronauts proudly wear the silver astronaut pin when dressed up for special events, like giving speeches, visiting really important people, or participating in ceremonies.

click

VIP ENTRANCE

Your Mission Is Go!

Special Skills

You may be an astronaut now, but you've still got work to do before you're ready to lift off. And that's what mission-specific training is all about.

not so fast!

Mission Training

Once the space agency decides on your mission, you'll be grouped with experienced astronauts who can help you work on the skills you'll need to succeed. You may be asked to do robotics, space walks, and research. And you'll have your own tasks during liftoff and landing, too. But you need to be patient: it might be two or three years before you're ready to take a space walk to fix a robotic arm outside the ISS.

The *Apollo* astronauts who walked on the moon received training for geology fieldwork on the lunar surface.

Space-Walking Workout

The whole time you're learning to use tools in space or how to get into the foot restraints that space-walkers use to keep themselves in one place while working, you also need to keep fit. Here's how Dr. Dave does it:

* Stretch: gets you ready for exercise and helps prevent injuries.
* Warm-up (exercise bike): loosens those muscles.
* Aerobic exercise (40-minute run): works the heart and lungs.
* Strength and endurance training (75 minutes): builds bone and muscle.
* Cool down and stretch: avoids soreness and stiffness later on.

And don't forget your water bottle!

Astronaut Buzz Aldrin of *Apollo 11* on one of the first Extravehicular Activities (EVAs) on the surface of the Moon

Patch Me In!

Once your mission training is complete, you'll get your mission badge patches, your name tag patch, and the flag of your country sewn onto your space suit. Almost ready to blast off!

Waiting for Weightlessness

Not assigned to a spaceflight right away? That's okay—there's still a lot to do. You could be asked to help out with ongoing mission operations. Maybe you'll

* help to develop robots for the ISS.
* take part in research or medical activities.
* become a "CAPCOM" (or capsule communicator). That's the person on the ground in mission control who talks to the astronauts.

A view of the shuttle flight control room

No YOU look like a dot!

Astronaut Cady Coleman with Robonaut 2, a robot astronaut helper

A Golden Landing

Once you finally make it to space and home again, you'll have tons of amazing memories to remind you of your trip. But you'll have another very special reminder, too: a gold version of the astronaut pin is flown on your first flight and is presented to you after landing.

Being assigned to a mission is like getting a present you've been wanting for a really long time. It's exciting— but it can also be scary!

Onward and Upward

Astronauts keep learning—even when they finally blast off. On-orbit training happens during a mission and helps you stay focused and ready. If you're about to tackle a robotic repair, you want to be sure you know just what to do. And if you're the medical officer (and your training was almost a year ago), regular review will keep you ready to stitch up a crewmate's cut.

Mission Muscles

Not all on-orbit training is about skills. Exercise is also very important. Astronauts work out up to two hours a day. Imagine landing on Mars after six months of space travel and falling down the ladder because your muscles are not strong enough! Astronauts use the Advanced Resistive Exercise Device (ARED) to strengthen muscles and the treadmill or cycle ergometer to stay in shape.

Astronaut Chris Cassidy uses the ARED to work out on the ISS.

In space, I used the exercise bike to cycle around Earth in 90 minutes—the time it takes a spacecraft to orbit our planet!

Astronaut Sunita Williams ran a marathon while in orbit.

Keep on Training!

So now you know what it takes to be an astronaut. It takes curiosity and commitment, passion and resilience, and a willingness to continue learning new (and tricky!) skills.

Astronaut, pro athlete, doctor, scientist, or rock star—whether you go to space or pursue your dreams on Earth, training like an astronaut will help you be the best you can be.

Class of 2066

FURTHER READING

Cunti, Loredana (Author), Williams, Dave (Author), and Krynauw, Theo (Illustrator), *To Burp or Not To Burp: A Guide to Your Body In Space*, Annick Press, 2016.

Esbaum, Jill. *Little Kids First Big Book of How*, National Geographic Kids Books, 2016.

Long, Denise. *Survivor Kid: A Practical Guide to Wilderness Survival*, Chicago Review Press, 2011.

O'Brien, Patrick. *You Are the First Kid on Mars*, Putnam Juvenile, 2009.

ONLINE RESOURCES

CANADIAN SPACE AGENCY—ACTIVITIES
www.asc-csa.gc.ca/eng/multimedia/activities/default.asp

EUROPEAN SPACE AGENCY—ESA KIDS
www.esa.int/esaKIDSen/

NASA KIDS CLUB
www.nasa.gov/kidsclub

IMAGE CREDITS

INDEX

We acknowledge the support of the Canada Council for the Arts, the Ontario Arts Council, and the participation of
the Government of Canada/la participation du gouvernement du Canada for our publishing activities.

Funded by the Government of Canada · Financé par le gouvernement du Canada | Canada

ONTARIO ARTS COUNCIL
CONSEIL DES ARTS DE L'ONTARIO
an Ontario government agency
un organisme du gouvernement de l'Ontario

Cataloging in Publication

Williams, Dafydd, 1954-, author
Go for liftoff! : how to train like an astronaut /
Dr. Dave Williams and Loredana Cunti.

(Dr. Dave, astronaut)
Issued in print and electronic formats.
ISBN 978-1-55451-914-9 (paperback).–ISBN 978-1-55451-915-6 (hardback).–
ISBN 978-1-55451-917-0 (pdf).–ISBN 978-1-55451-916-3 (epub)
1. Astronauts–Training of–Juvenile literature. 2. Astronautics–
Vocational guidance–Juvenile literature. I. Cunti, Loredana, 1968-, author
II. Title. III. Series: Williams, Dafydd, 1954-. Dr. Dave, astronaut

TL850.W56 2017   j629.45'07   C2016-906255-4
                                            C2016-906256-2

Published in the U.S.A. by Annick Press (U.S.) Ltd.
Distributed in Canada by University of Toronto Press.
Distributed in the U.S.A. by Publishers Group West.

Printed in China

Visit us at: www.annickpress.com

Also available in e-book format. Please visit www.annickpress.com/ebooks.html for more details.
Or scan